SOCIAL MEDIA MARKETING FOR MUSICIANS THAT WORKS!

A GUIDE TO BREAKING THE CYCLES OF EVERYTHING YOU ARE DOING WRONG.
(AND YES, YOU ARE DOING IT ALL WRONG)

DAN SHINDER

Copyright: Published in the United States by Dan Shinder
© Daniel R. Shinder **2018**
Published by Shindig Publishing

All rights reserved. No part of this publication may be reproduced, stored in retrieval system, copied in any form or by any means, electronic, mechanical, photocopying, recording or otherwise transmitted without written permission from the publisher. Please do not participate in or encourage piracy of this material in any way. You must not circulate this book in any format. Dan Shinder does not control or direct users' actions and is not responsible for the information or content shared, harm and/or actions of the book readers.

In accordance with the U.S. Copyright Act of 1976, the scanning, uploading and electronic sharing of any part of this book without the permission of the publisher constitute unlawful piracy and theft of the author's intellectual property. If you would like to use material from the book (other than just simply for reviewing the book), prior permission must be obtained by contacting the author at dan@socialmediamartketingformusicians.com

Thank you for your support of the author's rights.

CONTENTS

Acknowledgments 5

Forward 7

Introduction 9

Chapter 1: Whom your content is for 13

Chapter 2: The formula for fabulous content 21

ACKNOWLEDGMENTS

It's difficult to narrow a list like this down, yet at the same time there are certain individuals who clearly stand out to me whom I must acknowledge. Some fairly new to my life, some life-long.

First and absolutely foremost is my wife and Life-Mate, Nja Onê ("En-jah Oh-nee"). How this amazing woman has put up with me for 10 years+ so far, let along since I started Drum Talk TV since January, 2013 and subsequently Social Media On Steroids is a mystery. Without her support, I could never have accomplished any of what I have.

I would like to thank Bob Pike, CSP,CPAE who inspired me to create this Kindle Short series and guided me through the process of making it happen.

Thank you Jim Plouffe for your gifts of phenomenal reads which have sparked the writing fire under my butt and for the one-liner of some of the best wisdom I can ever share (it's in this book!).

Thank you to Drum Talk TV Fans everywhere for following what we do and for all the support and thank you to my right hand man at Drum Talk TV, Steven Shinder.

Thanks to all our kids (His) Victoria, Sammantha, Alex, Steven (and hers), Kevon, Sudy, Aaliyah, Shahada, Jesse, Jarquan and Jessica.

And to Lori Shube, who was not only my partner for the first 3 ½ years at three months in, but is a great friend who showed me I knew what I was doing, and what it meant, gave it context, language and definition.

Lastly and not least, I want to acknowledge **YOU** for wearing your business hat as a musician walking down this path trusting me!

FORWARD

Hi, I'm Linda Arcello-Earl, Manager of the band Foghat. Three years ago, myself and our social media manager took one of Dan's very cool social media marketing courses as part of his Social Media On Steroids series. Although we were pretty good at social media, Dan was able to teach us to streamline our efforts and maximize our reach. We applied what we learned to help market a crowd funding campaign through Pledge Music for our 2016 album "Under The Influence" and we had a great response from fans. We have continued to apply techniques we learned to help us grow our audience on social media and drive traffic to our websites.

It's great that Dan is encapsulating so much information in this 10-volume Kindle Short series. Dan has extensive knowledge in the social media marketing realm and if you are a musician, artist, music educator—anyone in the music space looking to grow your online following and have them engage with you, I highly recommend you to read this series and apply what you learn!

Rock on!

-Linda Arcello-Earl
Foghat
Noisy S.O.D. Management, Inc.

INTRODUCTION

Congratulations - Really!

You are being congratulated simply because if you are going down the path of seriously learning and applying my proven social media marketing strategies, this is a HUGE step, especially if you are in the arts; especially if you are a musician or music educator.

Quick story:
While I have taught, consulted and provided the service of my exceptionally effective social media marketing strategies from my "Social Media On Steroids" products and services to 100's of people in the arts, primarily musicians from garage bands, to Gold and Platinum Artists, educators and everyone in-between, at one point I pulled the plug on dealing with my own tribe. This was *painful* to me! But I had run out of places on my office walls to bang my head against at the frustration of how many musicians either thought they didn't need it or just didn't want to learn it or put in the work it takes to get results. Don't let the word "work" scare you away. The work is easy, and I will teach you the strategies I have used to grow the Drum Talk TV following to over 1 Million fans 100% organically—and still use! I tell people, *"it's so easy, even a drummer can do it! If I can do it, you can do it!"*

And even if you are thinking, "I don't really need a million fans" (and I am not sure how that could hurt), would 10,000 new active fans help whatever you are doing? Would 50,000? 150,000? 250,000? Of course it would and I used the same strategies to cross all these milestones, and I am going to share them with you, beginning with *"Essentials You Need To Know"* in this Volume I of X.

I have also worked with multimillionaire entrepreneurs, new start-ups, large corporations and the strategies are really all the same. However, this 10-volume series is designed especially for the community I come from, the music community. So what happened? Why did I circle back to my tribe?

Not to sound too sappy, mushy or cheesy, but honestly, I care. Really. The reason I began teaching all this back in the first year of Drum Talk TV when we began getting exceptional results organically and I knew I had something to share. By the way, "organically" means without spending money on advertising, "buying Likes," or boosting posts.

After having a lot of success with clients outside the music industry (and I mean *a lot!*), this made me want to share this knowledge with the music community that much more, even if I practically had to just give it away. And that's risky, because sometimes people have a perception that something doesn't have value if it's free or very inexpensive. I am willing to take a chance in this case, and congratulations again that you are too! I guarantee that if you apply exactly what I teach, you will get better results than you ever have with your social media marketing.

So before we begin, here are a few sprinkles of encouragement, inspiration, motivation, tips and advice for moving forward:

Many people "teach" social media marketing, though I have seen almost none who have proof of great results using what they teach. The ones that do seem to not teach *how* they got great results. I have exceptional results and teach exactly how I have done this.

A friend of mine and client, Jim Plouffe, has a great saying on his website:

*Never take advice from someone
who hasn't done what you want to do!*

If growing your online following, increasing online engagement and driving traffic is any part of what you want to do, guess what, you've come to the right guy.

You need to have the willingness to fail in order to succeed, but you need to have the context to know you are failing. Otherwise, you will never know what to adjust in order to succeed.

When you think you know it all ... that's all you know.

Focus on "Progress, Not Perfection," as Author Bob Pike, one of my mentors tells me. I agree, and perfection (if there is such a thing), can come with time. Whereas, **you need progress NOW!**

Understand that this one volume, let alone the entire series of ten, is about much more than growing a following, creating engagement and driving traffic.

It's about creating trust, likeability and brand love. This is what you need, not mere page "Likes" or "Followers" as statistics. You are going to be providing an experience as a brand with each channel and each post! What you will do will have so much meaning that even in any small way for moments at a time, what you provide will become part of your fans' lifestyle! If what you post is not worthy of that, it's not worthy of being a post. It's gibberish... or narcissism ... or you are just barfing out thoughts believing everyone thinks it's cool. I guess all of that is the same, but you have SO MUCH MORE TO OFFER!

And I am going to show you how to show this to your target market. Yes, there are few business terms woven into this as well, and even a bit of ...

When people ask me in interviews, or when I am asked to do a key note speech, or in conversation, "What's the main granular ingredient to successful social media marketing?" I tell them:

Love what you do and get others to fall in love with being part of it.

Accomplish this and your social media marketing is a success.

-Dan Shinder
Founder/CEO of Drum Talk TV

CHAPTER 1
WHOM YOUR CONTENT IS FOR

It's All For Them!

First, I want to be very clear that I will always speak [type] with 100% honesty, I am always straight forward and say things in a way I truly hope will resonate with you, strike a nerve, reach your sensibilities, inspire you, motivate you – whatever it takes to getting the best work out of you and say it the only way I know how. This is for you, not for me. Sometimes it may come off as pompous, conceded, cavalier, or snarky, but it always it the truth and it always directed to you with love and the best intensions.

So, we're cool, right?

Good. Now let's *ROCK* our social media marketing!!!

Everything I teach comes from getting exceptional results that NO ONE in the music space is getting but us. And for the first 4 ½ years, I was the only one creating, curating and scheduling the content, yet within the first year, our reach and engagement was 900% greater than our industry peers all combined. Without naming them, this includes all the print magazines that cover the world of drumming and their online presences, as well as a couple that already are only online. I *knew* I had something to share.

The following graphic is a 7-day report taken Dec. 7, 2017 the day we turned 1 Million on the "Likes" odometer on the Drum Talk TV Facebook page, and "Followers" (which is more important) turned 1 Million shortly thereafter and has grown at a faster pace.

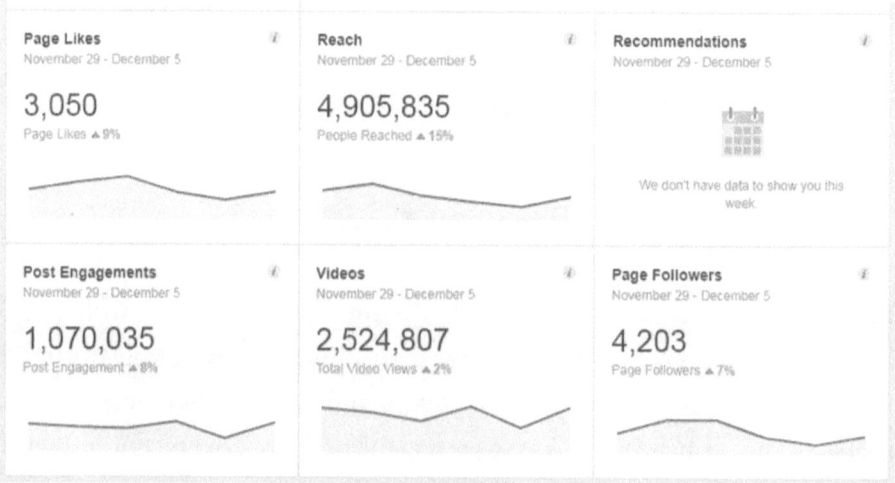

And to show that you do not need a million followers to get great results, the screenshot below is from our 7th week, February 2013 with somewhat different statistics being reported, but you can still see exceptional results:

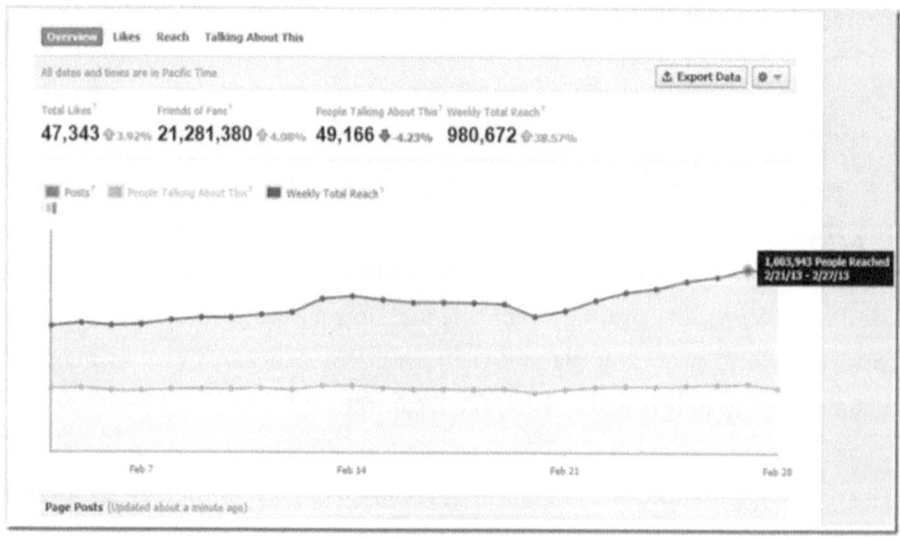

I always say, "You have got to get out of the box, get out of neutral and do something different to get better results!"

We've all heard the definition of insanity: Doing the same thing over and over and expecting a different result. Let's do something different.

If this chapter doesn't hit you over the head like a barrel of idea lightbulbs popping on, I don't know what will, so here we go!

I am going to start off by telling you the number one mistake virtually *every* brand is making with their weak attempts at social media marketing. And yes, musicians and music educators, you are a "brand." This error is not limited to the music industry. I am also referring to your favorite fortune 500 companies around the world.

Here is an example of what they are doing wrong with every post … and you likely are too, no offense:

Promote, Promote, **Promote,** Promote, *Promote, Promote, Promote,* Promote, *Promote, Promote, Promote,* **Promote,** *Promote,* **Promote,** *Promote, Promote,* Promote, *Promote, Promote,* Promote, *Promote, Promote, Promote,* **Promote,** *Promote, Promote, Promote, Promote, Promote,* Promote, *Promote,* **Promote,** *Promote, Promote, Promote, Promote, Promote, Promote,* **Promote!!!**

Yep, that's what it looks like. A few different flavors, scents and textures mixed in, but that's about how it looks. All they do is "Promote" with virtually every post … and you might be too.

(Ha-ha, "might be"???)

You may ask, "Well, what's wrong with that? This is why I established social media channels for my brand, so I can *promote!*"

Ah yes, makes sense from an instinctive point of view, but does not make sense strategically. Nor does it work, ever. You cannot build a community around a brand by constantly promoting. This is completely non-inclusive, and your target market will not become fans in love with what you do unless you make them a part of it. This means NOT jamming down their throats what you are selling with every freaking post!

So, to look at it from the outside in, just for clarity, think of it this way: As a band or artist, if all you posted was messaging that said, "Buy our shirt, Buy our CD, Download our single, Come to our show" over and over, how do you imagine building a fan base around that? And what if they *did* buy your shirt, buy your CD, download your single and go to your show … *then* what???

I am not saying not to promote, I am saying that success in building an online fan base in love with—or at least interested in—what you do requires content designed *FOR THEM*. This should be about 80% of your content, or at least 70%. Let's shoot for 80% and call it the 80/20 rule. This 80/20 rule = 80% of your total social media marketing content is "community-building" content, while the remaining 20% is for promoting/marketing/sales, etc.

So this is what you want to avoid being perceived as:

Would you watch that channel? Would you listen to a radio station that played a song at the top and bottom of the hour and was 25 minutes of commercials in-between? Of course not, so don't run your social media channels that way!

Here's a BIG lesson to help get your head around looking a creating content a whole new way:

Facts Tell, but Stories Sell.
Social Media Marketing is All About Storytelling.
Love what you do and get others to fall in love with being part of it.

Your Content is for Your Target Market, not you.

It's to convert them to Fans of Your Brand and to KEEP THEM as Fans so *they* spread the word.

Imagine that! OTHER PEOPLE championing your brand *for* you! Allow me to illustrate how important this is:

I can run around all day saying how great Drum Talk TV is or Social Media On Steroids, but who is going to listen to me? Of COURSE I am going to say that! But when fans of your brand, your audience, your students whomever you serve runs around saying how great your brand is—your music, your music lessons, your baked beans—whatever, THAT is worth its weight in gold, *literally!*

So remember, what you post cannot just be promoting what you do if you want to build a community of people in love with what you are offering.

Right about now people ask bewilderedly, "What else do we post???" This is where it gets really fun! Here's the answer:

> **Post exceptional content to share with your audience that matters to _them_.**

But what the heck does *that* mean???

It really means that it's time to sit at the grown-ups table and be objective about your material to ensure it accomplishes the above. And this is THEE most important skill you can develop as a content marketer, which you now are. You need to be objective and not just rely on your friends, who with all good intentions will hold your hand as they walk with you smiling and nodding all the way to the cliff until you drop off telling you how cool your sh#t is ... and it's not.

But don't worry, I have a formula that will put you on the fast track to develop these skills and check your work against until it becomes habitual and instinctive so you can avoid this the next time you launch something ...

[Is there anybody ... *OUT THERE?*]

CHAPTER 2
THE FORMULA FOR FABULOUS CONTENT

(And it ALWAYS has to be Fabulous!)

Another quick story to get you primed on this topic:

When I first started Drum Talk TV, I had in mind I would blog. It would be natural to do that, right? I was always thinking of topics to blog about, and I would get excited! But then I would get busy and the blogging slid down the priority list. I went though this cycle for three years until I realized, "Wait a minute. I don't feel compelled to blog because I am already doing on social media what the experts say blogging should accomplish." And this is what I call "Five to Keep Your Brand Alive." Every post must, must, must include one or more of the following elements to help you create content to convert lookers into fans (and then fans into buyers):

1. Stay Present
2. Stay Relevant
3. Be Inclusive
4. Be Helpful to Others
5. Be Seen as an Expert in Your Field

ALL without *selling!* Use this as a content quality control checklist and you are golden, I promise! However, it is important to understand that there is more to the equation. The more of my proven strategies you incorporate into your social media marketing, the better you get at it and the sooner your results will improve.

On the subject of results, know that I will close Volume I with very clear instruction on what results are, regardless of what social media marketing platforms you are using. But basically, what we are looking to do constantly is reach more people of our target market, as well as influencers (people who may not exactly be your core target market but know or are related to people who are), get more engagement, and get more click through's, even if you aren't selling anything yet. What??? Ah-Ha, let's talk about that for a moment.

Another quick story!

This one is great because it illustrates how important it is to build an audience NOW and not wait until your next gig, or until you begin selling lessons, or until your next CD is out, or downloadable, or book, or DVD or product or whoo-joo-widgitz ... *DO IT NOW!!!*

The above is a common mistake many people in business make (yes, you're in business). I can't tell you how many people turned down taking even free webinars I gave teaching this stuff because they said, "But I don't have anything to promote."

HUH???

They were bands, artists and educators. They thought that because they didn't have a new CD out yet, for example, they had no reason to build an audience. Then when they DID have a CD to release, they did so to crickets and tumble weeds, *because they didn't build a fan base first in love with who they are!*

Just promote it and they will buy. Yeah right.

Before I show you a grotesque, yet true story of this scenario here's one from my history:

Before I started Drum Talk TV, I had an online lesson platform called "Dan's Drum Clinics." I was actually very new to social media (June 2012). My thought was that I wanted to offer free online lessons and eventually have paid subscription-based levels. It made sense to me from the very beginning that what I needed more than anything was a following It didn't matter how good my lessons were if there was no one watching. Before I released my first lesson, I had followers from 64 countries, 100% organically!

I hardly knew what social media marketing was, but I knew this much made sense. So what did I post? Drummers birthdays, drummer's quotes, artists drum solos, even lessons by other educators and a lot of people thought I was crazy! "Why would you post your competitor's lessons?" they would ask. It never occurred to me that I should be in competition with anyone.

Fast-Forward six months when I started Drum talk TV (and here comes the gold), I knew that no matter how big an artist, educator or maker of gear was, or how great our interviews were, or how slick the post production was (we're still working on all that), none of that mattered if nobody was watching.

I also knew that our interviews might not be the only thing people would be interested in, and that they may be the *least* of what they were interested in. This required sitting at the grown-ups table and realizing that we needed all sorts of other types of content to share to our audience besides just our core products: Interviews, event coverage and documentaries.

This means that no matter how good your product or service is—no matter what you are offering—none of it matters at all if you don't have a constantly growing fan base in love with what you do.

So here's the thing, you don't need people who just click Like on your facebook page. Our 1 Million plus Likes would mean nothing if we didn't have a high level of engagement.

"Likes" don't buy tickets to shows. Likes don't scream their favorite song out at your gig. Likes don't share your awesome video (which I will teach you how to make shareable in another Volume of this series), Likes don't buy concert shirts or other swag, Likes don't sign up for lessons. LIKES DON'T DO SH#T!!! Real fans and customers do. So what you need is fans of your brand.

And where that begins is with Brand Awareness, which requires Reach.

SOCIAL MEDIA MARKETING FOR MUSICIANS THAT WORKS!

(That's a lot of people with different colored skin and shirts, not M&M's, marshmallows and chocolate chips on a graham cracker)

And with Great Content you will create Trust, Likeability and Brand Love. And then they will buy … or sign up or do whatever it is your need/goal for them to do is.

Content, Content, Content, it's all about the content and it's got to be for *THEM!*

I mentioned one other illustration of how important it is to build a community around your brand, and I mentioned this was grotesque yet true example, so buckle in …

True Story:
A man had an idea for a drumming accessory product. We'll call him John because that's his name. However, even though this is public information, I will not use his company or product name and have blurred out his failed crowdfunding campaign graphic. If you know who it is, again, no big deal, it's

public info. Anyhow, John came to me to tell me about his product and the fact that he was going to have a booth at the 2017 Winter NAMM Show and was going to do a crowdfunding campaign right away because he *had* to raise a lot on money *now!*

The first thing I did was look at his Facebook fan page for his brand and can you guess what was missing? That's right, the "crowd" he was going to run a crowdfunding campaign to.

I told him this and told him I had the answer to show him how to build an enormous crowd *in love* with his product's concept and the problem it would solve. Sensitive to the fact that he was a new start-up and needed this to happen to raise money, I offered him a ridiculously discounted price for my expertise.

But John said no. John said there was no time to learn this stuff and put it into action. He needed to raise many now and he believed in the goodness of his heart and from the encouragement of a few friends that all he had to do was run a Kickstarter campaign, which is all or nothing, by the way, and people would throw money at him until he had the $19,000 goal he needed.

Here's where he ended up with his "Make your goal or you get nothing" Kickstarter campaign:

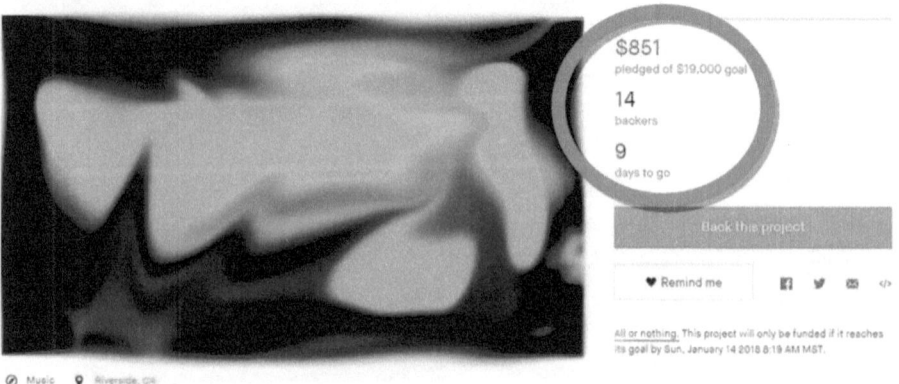

With nine days to go he had $851 of his $19,000. At the end of those last nine days, he still had less than $1,000. Why? Because he didn't build a crowd and create trust, likeability and brand love around his brand. Even with only 1,493 page likes, all he needed was $12.73 per person to reach his goal. But he couldn't even do that because he had no relationship with his "audience."

John had this:

But he needed this.

What do you have?

This isn't to shame anyone; it's an example of what works and what does not. All he did was post over and over, essentially, "Give me money! Give me money! Give me money! Give me money!" and that is all anyone is doing if all they do is create posts that only promote what they are offering.

So what's the answer?

Post exceptional content to share with your audience that matters to *them*.

You need to post about 80% Community-Building Material and 20% you blatantly promoting what you have going on. We are going to concentrate on the **80%** for now.

So are you ready for some great content ideas? Let's Rock!

OK, step one:

Who is your target audience? This is important to understand that it cannot just be a bunch of the same people under the same umbrella. That can absolutely be part of it, but not the whole. We need to get more granular than that. So let's do an exercise to drill down to your target market because this will help identify what content to create to ensure you are creating content that will help you:

1. **Stay Present**
2. **Stay Relevant**
3. **Be Inclusive**
4. **Be Helpful to Others**
5. **Be Seen as an Expert in Your Field**

The first thing you want to do is list the top five "Personas" your content will speak to. Let's say you are a band that plays classic rock. You want people who:

1. Love Classic Rock
2. Go to Concerts (at whatever level venues/functions you perform)
3. If you have a CD, you want to reach classic rock style lovers who buy CD's
4. If you have Downloads, same thing
5. For number five you can list people who love bands of the styles you play, or the fans of the bands you play if you do cover/tributes.

Get it so far?

If you are a music educator, basically fill in the same blanks with:

1. People who want to pay for lessons of whatever you teach (or parents who want to pay)
2. Fit your age demographics
3. Fit your level of play requirements, depending on who you teach
4. Are within a certain travel distance if you teach in person, or fit your profile for Skype/Zoom students
5. Want to learn the styles you are teaching

Step two:

Now that you have your target market figured out you can start listing content. I am going to give you ideas for content to get your creative juices flowing—yes, you get to be creative with the business side—and then I am going to give you important formulas to follow to make sure your posts are created as effectively as can be. But let's stay on this roll for now.

Going back to the band that plays classic rock style music (and fill in the blanks to fit whatever you do), you would post news, articles, video clips, photos and your own stories of the people whose music you play, or if your music is all original, the artists whom have influenced you. Right there is 5 content ideas for each member of the band. If you have 4 people in your group, that's 20 posts right off the bat. Hello??? Is this thing on??? Let's move on and I'll blow your mind with content ideas for dozens of posts! DOZENS!!!

Buckle in more tightly, here we go—and this is for each member of the band, and works for individual artists and music educators as well. In no particular order you can post about:

1. Your first gear
2. Your Current Gear
3. The first album you got of your favorite genre
4. What/Who got you into music
5. Your favorite player of your primary instrument
6. Your first or biggest musical influence (they may not be the same as #5 or each other)
7. Your most recent "record" purchase
8. Your most recent contemporary influence
9. Your first concert
10. Your most recent concert
11. Your favorite concert and why
12. The furthest you traveled for a concert
13. Whom you would love to spend a week studying with on your instrument
14. The most challenging thing you ever learned on your instrument
15. The first thing you learned on your instrument
16. The most recent thing you learned on your instrument

17. The least amount of people you performed for
18. The most amount of people you performed for
19. Your Dream Venue to perform at
20. Your Dream Band to Tour with

Getting the picture??? That's 20 post ideas x's 4 band members, for example is 80 post ideas for the 80% category NOT jamming down your fans' throats what you are promoting. But why is this necessary? Why does this matter?

- This Builds Community.
- This Builds Likeability.
- This Builds Trust.
- This Builds Brand Love.
- This Builds a Relationship with your target market; with your audience, and you neeeeeeed that. Right? Hopefully you learned that so far to the degree that you believe it, understand it and are willing to earn it.

So next time you wonder what the heck to post for your 80%, remember this tip of the iceberg of an abundance of material right in your own experience, and that's really the point. Think about it as a music fan yourself: getting to know musicians, artists and educators you admire. How cool is that? Give your fans the same opportunity, they will eat it all up, I promise. Especially ... if you include them! Here's how:

Simply ask them the same question you are posting about. This leads us to the three magic ingredients virtually EVERY POST MUST HAVE, with the exception of a meme most the time, which I will explain in another volume.

Ready for the magic three? Follow me ...

Virtually every post must have the following three ingredients and I guarantee if you do this consistently, your numbers will change tremendously and pretty much immediately. They are:

1. **A Question**
2. **A Description**
3. **A Call to Action**

Let's break down why by showing what happens with the "what if" you do this.

A **Question** is an invitation to participate. It gives permission. It's almost impossible not to get answers if you ask a question, and it should almost always go first to pique interest and get them involved right from the start. There's your engagement. You're welcome.

The **Description** gives you the opportunity to not only describe the video or image in the post (duh), but it's your chance to implement the storytelling aspect of the post. Today's social media marketing is all about storytelling. You've got to tell the story, otherwise it's a big "So what?" (like maybe most the posts you are doing—errrrr—I mean seeing). Facts tell, but stories sell. Tell the story … *briefly*.

And the **Call to Action** is to give them something to do you will both benefit from, such as sign up for a newsletter, check your gig schedule, check your sample lessons … soft-selling, not the 20% blatant selling category. In fact, on Facebook especially, there's a caveat to doing this the most effective way, and that is to not use third-party links that will take the viewer off of Facebook.

So what we do at Drum Talk TV for most the 80% content category posts is this:

We send them to our videos album on our Facebook page for them to fall down a rabbit hole of content, most of which they never saw and it gives all that much more reason to fall in love with our brand. Here's how that call to action reads:

STAY inspired! See more fun, inspiring drumming/percussion videos from over 130 countries around the world at www.facebook.com/DrumTalkTV/videos

It's that simple. In a future volume, I will go deeper into the many algorithms in place to thwart your reach and show you how to legitimately and ethically get around them.

By the way, you have GOT to have a Facebook Fan Page. This is a must. Don't even question it. Well, you can, but I will give the top reasons as to why you need this …

1. It's the biggest platform with about 2 BILLION monthly users. 62% of all consumers are on Facebook. It's the largest platform available to reach the most amount of people, period. And here's a bit of perspective: Only 12% of all consumers use Pinterest, only 11% use Twitter and only 9% use Instagram. ONLY NINE!!! (as of this writing, May 2018)
2. FB has virtually every bell, whistle, feature, function, benefit, app, etc. that all the other platforms have rolled into one.
3. Like it or not, it's where all the people are. Yes, even the millennials, even the 18-24 year-olds.

If you are not on Facebook because of "the drama," you have other problems. Get over it. People who have drama on social media have drama in their real life; at the bank, in the restaurant, at work, at the grocery store, in their relationships. Stop blaming Facebook.

What I teach can work for any platform. It's more about the human behavior than it is the tools. When your head is completely around that and what really constitutes as great content, that's when you will be a winner, I promise. There's no way it can't work.

Remember what Jim Plouffe's advice is?

Never take advice from someone who hasn't done what you want to do!

I have done everything I have taught you so far and it works. There is SO much more to all this, but this first volume of this series will give you more of start than most fortune 500 companies know how to do.

The number one thing to always keep in mind when creating content? Wear the fan's hat … use as much objectivity as possible.

Be sure each post hits points of "5 to Keep Your Brand Alive":

1. **Stay Present**
2. **Stay Relevant**
3. **Be Inclusive**
4. **Be Helpful to Others**
5. **Be Seen as an Expert in Your Field**

Lastly, let's be clear on what "Results" in social media marketing are. Getting results means you are growing your audience weekly at an increasing level, at least for a while, and then consistently.

Getting results also means getting engagement, real engagement. Taking Facebook, for example, "Likes" on a post mean *nothing*, absolutely zero. You can't learn anything from them. One may argue that it shows me how many people "like" my post, but not really. Think of how easy it is to click that little button as you speed scroll down the newsfeed.

You want comments and shares. Comments are where you learn about your audience and where you humanize the experience by interacting with them; Answering questions; Responding to their comments; thanking them.

Shares are where you grow. Follow the steps I gave you to creating more effective content and your fans will share it. In a future volume of this series I will share with you how we spread our content from our on channel without spending money to boost posts. It will work for you too.

Looking at Facebook insights on the following page as an example, I show the order of priority of what matters.

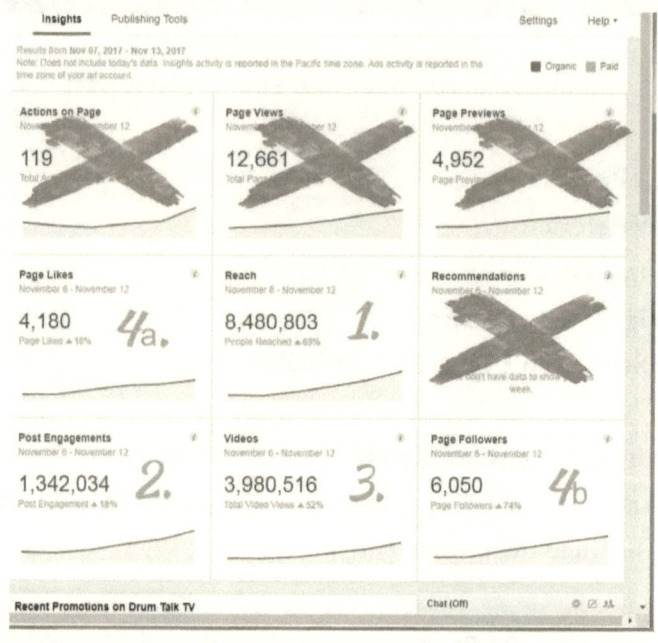

X = No value in these stats whatsoever.

Actions on Page are how many people checked the contact info on your page. Doesn't mean anything.

Page Views mean nothing. People see your page's content in their newsfeed, it doesn't matter how many people come to your page. Remember, the smartest thing to do is to have calls to action driving people to your videos album to see everything they have missed and fall down that rabbit hole, commenting and sharing, generating engagement.

Page Previews is when someone hovers over a link to your page and sees a preview of your pages preview image. So what? Worthless stat!

1 = It all begins with reach. Yes, posts need to have certain ingredients to perform, but brand awareness is the biggest item, this is where you get your fans from.

2 = Post Engagements mean you have REAL FANS, not just page likes. Comments and shares are THEE most important part of this stat. Comments are where you learn from your audience and build the relationship with your fans and where you learn from them and see what's working and what is not.

3 = Video Views are the third most important stat. The more views you have the more you know people are paying attention, interested and this is achieving brand awareness and engagement at the same time. You know your message is getting out there and doing something.

4 = This stat is more important than page "Likes." These are people who have clicked "Follow" on your page in the seven-day period of the report; they show your new "followers" for that period to theoretically ensure they get your posts in their newsfeed. It's what most people *think* a page "like" is.

5 = This is simply a statistic that shows how many people clicked "Like" on your page for that seven-day period. It doesn't mean they see your content, it doesn't tell you whether or not they like it or care, it's tells you nothing. The only reason it is not in the red X category is because the entire world *THINKS* this stat means something, so there is a perception value factor, that's all.

So, time to get to work! Get used to using all of this every day and move onto the next Volume(s) so you can learn more, be that much better and get even greater results!

Go to www.SocialMediaMarketingForMusicians.com to stay up to date as new volumes get released, or reach out via dan@advancedsocialmarketing.com if you are interested in one of my courses.

To your success!

www.ingramcontent.com/pod-product-compliance
Lightning Source LLC
Chambersburg PA
CBHW031513210526
45464CB00007B/2892